This Book is written in a time of need. Things are not as they used to be…This world we live in needs to stop… and look around at what she has become… what she wants us to become… and what we have chosen to be…

A Book of Poetry
"Poetry is an Art"

David X. Austin

Copyright Year: 2007
Copyright Notice: by David X. Austin.

All rights reserved. No part of this book may be reproduced in any form or by any means without the prior written consent of the publisher, excepting brief quotes used in interviews

Results in this copyright notice:

ISBN: 978-0-6151-7287-3

© *2007 by David X. Austin.*

Contents

1. Could you love me
2. Honesty
3. True love
4. Can it be true?
5. One special day
6. That love shit
7. Always
8. The thought that counts
9. Why I love you
10. Emotions
11. As I contemplate
12. Merry Christmas from Heaven
13. Let me Lean on you
14. Special Outings
15. Holidays are here
16. Women of need
17. Mold my heart
18. The eternal bond
19. Best wishes
20. Pedals in the wind
21. Angel
22. Four seasons

23. My contemplation
24. Being in love
25. A love so sweet
26. Poetry in motion
27. A good woman
28. Promise
29. Things to think about
30. A Black President
31. If he were here

\<Could you Love me?\>

I had a dream the other night

Where I woke up in a fright,

You and I were waiting there

Our hands were clasped you looked despaired,

The nurse and Doctor standing near

Holding something small and dear,

The infinite music from the bundle

Made my heart beat quick as thunder

A boy or girl was not determined

But the Lord has blessed our persons.

You are week from exhaustion

Sweating like a leaky faucet

Perspiration took its toll on you

My love I'll stay until were through.

Now you're sleep to no surprise

I kissed you soft upon your eyes

As I watch you're sleeping state

My heart begins to escalate

I woke up in a violent sweat

Reality hit I had regrets.

I only wish that you could see

How pure a love could truly be,

My dreams an example of what I mean

Where we had made a family!!

April 30, 2005
By David A.

\<Honesty\>

Maybe it's the things I say
Or maybe it's just me,
Yet all the women I ever loved
Have turned away from me.
That's why I try and write my feelings
In my poetry.
I barely write my letters
With all my heart you see
For fear of losing, you my love
The closet one to me.
If ever I had, had the chance
To get on bended knee,
Don't think that I would hesitate
To ask you as my queen.
The fear is not in the commitment
But in your reply.
I am kneeling here staring you
Directly in your eye!
Because the next few words you say
Will change you life and
Mine!!

5/11/03   David A.

"True Love"

This poem is written from a pen
Filled with kisses
If you love me answer me this,
Do you love me or isn't this so
Because if you don't I'd like to know
Yet if you do please tell me true
So I can tell you I love you too
And if I die before you do
I'll go to heaven and wait for you
If your not there on Judgment day
I'll know you went the other way,
I'll give the angels back their wings
And risk the loss of everything
I'll go to hell to be with you
To show you that my love is
True!!

3/6/03
David X. Austin

'Can it be true?'

I love to look up in the sky
Where things look peaceful in my eyes,
I sing the tunes of certain songs
That always makes me cry,
I'd love to look you in your eyes
And see the world just pass us by,
I'd hate to ever bring to you
The state of compromise,
I'd love to give you gifts of art
And love you deep within my heart,
I also wish that if together
We would never part,
As I wrote this rhyme to you
I had some time to think it through,
There must be something I can do
To show you that my
Love is true!!

3/21/03
David A.

'One Special Day'

I sit in such a dreamless state
And try to pick the perfect date,
On which I plan to give to you
All the joy a man can muse,
Candle lights and soften tunes
All the things to set the mood,
A dinner that was succulent
A kiss before I tuck you in,
I do not wish to break the vibe
By trying to get between your thighs,
If there's something you need of me
Don't hesitate to ask my queen,
Baby this is all for you
A day on which your dreams come
True!!

3/25/03
David X. Austin

"That Love Shit"

What of it! I put out and get burnt in return, soul mate of myself.

I shoved aside your past but yet mine to remain an obstacle thrown in my face every chance you get.

See that steals my Joy, my happiness-

-That Love Shit-

I pray to my higher power that we together because strong in his word- yet my emotions are still treated at that of a sugar daddy, uncared for, don't care about, you care less-need I say more? Need I point out the pain galore, the tears that pour, that angel white wing over my problems no longer soars.

-That Love Shit-

You swore this and that and I believed you

And you, and you, and you, and you!!!

See that's how many bitches destroyed a part of me. I'm keeping it real, letting you know that thugs cry too and when it happens- he had to be in love because crying is something thugs rarely do…

And I'm done, caput, finished, I quit! Crying over some chick

-That Love Shit-

11/21/02
David Austin

Always

It was the simple things that meant so much just the holding of hands I knew I was protected. Your smile subliminally stated everything-I was loved I was cared for, I was yours and it's to be <u>us</u> through eternity and beyond. See, you're not gone because I'm still in love, and you're still here because I see you as plain as day in my dreams and memory will do just fine you rest within me not R.I.P. Always

Those romantic walks are forever embedded in my heart and our talks, my eyes still sometimes weep for your gentleness that you kept from the world to see. And I'm sure my prayers were answered, because the time we shared was enough to last a lifetime for me. And now "He" lays <u>you</u> down to sleep I pray to my higher power that your soul he'll keep

Always

11/21/02   David A.

\<The Thought That Counts\>

I love to think of all the things
You've ever said to me,
Then lock them in my memory
For just mine eyes to see,
I wish I could express to you
All my thanks and gratitude,
I also make a vow to you
On everything I love to do,
I know at times I make mistakes
But it's your heart I'll never break,
I'll have it in a special place
Inside my heart like key and safe,
I love to send these cards to you
To show my thoughts are still on
You!

May 20, 2003
David Austin

-Questions-

Is there a love so pure and divine which could make my
heart beat in three quarter time,
A love that's so deep and would flow through my soul
That when she is gone I'm no longer a whole,
A love that is peaceful with no compromise ,
We need not to worry of people with lies,
I need you to tell me be honest with me,
Do you think in your heart
You could ever love
Me?!

5/23/03

David X. Austin

"Why I Love You"

I love the awkwardness of your stare
I love the radiance of your hair,
There are things that you may do
To make my wildest dreams come true.
I love your wit your intellect
Your whole decorum deserves respect,
I love your rouge that comes in tact
But it's the peace that drives me back,
Your passion for fusion fruits
The aura that comes from your roots,
I know you see my love is true
These are the reasons I love you!!!

3/23/03
David X. Austin

Emotions

As I sit lonely my heart sheds a tear
I try to keep silent so no one can hear,
My body is cold & I begin to sweat
Could this be something that I could regret,
Telling the truth that I really love you
Is that a mistake or the best thing to do
The last thing I want is to ever lose you
I love, I like, and associate too
The truth is that
I'll always love
You!!

3/28/03
David X. Austin

\<As I Contemplate\>

I have these thoughts inside my mind
Which makes me wanna write these rhymes,
Although a day has not gone by
Without you placed inside my mind,
I'm resting here upon my bed
While thoughts of you just flood my head,
As they come one by one
I try to voice them with my tongue
Of all the women that are pure
You're the one I love for sure,
Before I lay my head to rest
I think of you with no regrets,
Truly would you be with me
If I'd asked you for my
Queen

3/28/03

David Austin

Merry Christmas from Heaven

I still hear the songs, I still see the lights,
I still feel your love, on cold winter nights.
I still share your hopes, and all of your cares,
I'll even remind you to say all your prayers.
I just want to tell you, you still make me proud
You stand head and shoulders, above all the crowds.
Keep trying each moment to stay in his grace
I came here before you to help set your place,
You don't have to be perfect all of the time
He's there when you slip when you continue to climb.
To my family and friends please be thankful today
I'm still close beside you in a new special way.
I love you all dearly so don't shed a tear
Cause I'm spending my Christmas with GOD this year.

2/17/03
David A.

"Let Me Lean on You"

Keep your eyes on me
Keep me in your sight,
Help me down the crooked road
Lead me to the light,
The road I'm on is dark
I'm not sure I know the way,
Yet with you beside me
I certainly won't go astray,
Protect me from the world
I know we'll make it through,
Give me all the strength I need
"Let me lean on you"

2/21/03
David Austin

Special Outings

There are things I'd love to do
As long as you accompany too,
Like the movies or the shore
Where we'll be alone for sure,
Disney world or Great adventure
Roller coasters of great dimensions,
Cotton candy Funnel cake
Bugs bunny impersonates,
Giant cookies and Snow cones
Mickey and Minnie sing alongs,
All of this can sound real great
As long as you come as my
Date!

May 10th 2003
By David A.

"Holidays are here"

Once again I have sat down
To write a poem this year,
The holidays have come again
And so have all the cheers,
Seasons come and seasons go
As we remain apart,
Since we are I send this poem
To you with all my heart,
I'd cherish all the love you'd give
And harness all the fears,
Cause holidays will come again
And so will all my
Tears!

12/22/2002
David X. Austin

\<Women of Need\>

How come men do crazy things
And women are so humble,
Men act like they know it all
And women act so subtle,
Men are very clumsy too
And women hardly fumble
Yet without women's special deeds
A man would not succeed!

May 11, 2003
David A.

<Mold My Heart>

Here it is
I'm letting you in
To touch the softest part
My heart,
You shape the mold
You know the art
It's in your hands
Now
Mold my heart

May 12, 2003
David A.

The Eternal Bond

Dedicated to Dwayne and Family

Time passes quickly-yet not quick enough,
Although I'm not with you-
Things still must be tough,
But you are my cousin-no brother you see,
I pray that there's nothin-
To take you from me,
I know that you're strong
But listen and take heed,
Being without family it's hard to succeed.
I know you are busy as people must be,
Could you just keep in touch
And send pictures to me?
In a world adventures and controversy,
I ask you stay focused on all of your needs,
Your girl needs you now as I do family,
I know your loves deep
And I'm all for sharing
Cause blood thicker than water
And there's no comparing
I just never again want to experience
What went on with KAREN!!

-Best Wishes-

Although your birthday's over
And these wishes are belated,
Hope it was a happy day
That you just celebrated,
And hope the year that's just ahead
Will turn out happy too,
For that's the way it should be
For someone as nice as you.

7/1/03
David A.

Pedals in the wind

Delicate, gentle, elegant...
Fresh as the morning dew, sweet as honey dripping from your fingertips...
Intense is the blossom deeper than the anticipation of the caress of your lips...
You love me... You love me not...
The pain, the joy, the cold, the hot...
Memories of secrets locked in our private box of passion...
Can our desire stand the test of adversity...
Or will the beauty of our pedals wither in the suns gaze...you love me...you love me not...
I embrace with glee, but tremble with despair...
I listen quietly for whisperers through the air...
The fundamental roots are you're till the end...
My dearest, please tell me...
Are your pedals in the wind?

6/22/03

David Austin

-Angel-

Lord God how can this be
A beautiful angel's been sent unto me
A sweet lady from above to whom
I will give all my love
You sent an angel to an undeserving man,
Yet I will love her best that I can,
I cannot offer you diamonds or pearls
But for you trust me the world would be yours.
This world is unfair for that I understand
But to have a prize so precious
To cherish one
MAN!!

6-25-03
David A.

"Four Seasons"

There are rivers
That I know,
Born of ice
And melting snow,
White with rapids
Swift to roar,
With no farms
Along the shore,
With no mill wheel
Ever turning,
In a cold
Relentless yearning
And no cattle
Come to drink
At a starred
And welcoming
Brink,

*Only deer
And bear and mink,
At the shallows
Come to drink,
Little paddles
Swift and light,
Flick the current
In their flight,
I have seen my
Heart beat high,
Watching with
Exalting eyes,
These poor rivers
That have known,
No will no purpose
But their own.*

6/28/03
David A

<My Contemplation>

Out of the dark that covers me
Like blankets through the night,
Your love is like a brilliant star
That's brightened up my life
Seasons come and seasons go
As we remain apart
So I send this poem and card
To you with all my heart.
A day has yet to have gone by
With out you on my mind
So I use my time to show you
That my love is true,
Cause till the day we meet again
My thoughts will be on
YOU!!

David
10/17/06

Being in Love...
The special friendship that can never be disturbed...
Have you ever been in love have you ever felt the feelings?
Being in Love...
That feeling like the lump in your throat, when you are so hurt that the pain is untouchable, the tears don't come
Being in Love...
The passion in the pain is unexplainable, incomparable, unreachable, understandable...
Being in Love...
The love in the feeling is impeccable, the uniqueness in the exotic way we make love, over the rainbow...
Being in Love...
Our bodies are compatible to the fullest extent of the laws of nature like sunshine, rainfall, thunder and lightning...
Being in Love...
*There is **NO** other way to explain the feeling that my mate gives me and I him...*
Being in Love...
We become one and the warmth of his strong arms around my body and soul, embracing my inner most feelings protecting me from any harm...
Being in Love...

His loving me like, I have never been loved before! Then hearing you say, **I Love you...** *and I you...*
**Damn!!!
Being in Love...**

**2/2004
By Anice Austin**

A Love So sweet

Come here darling have a seat we need to speak

Look straight into my eyes tell me what you see,

Am I the woman in your dreams, who slides out of her jeans you're digging everything about me is it as good as it seems? Gain your trust, boo that's a must. You're longing for my touch lay my head on your shoulder and let you know what's on my mind, good men are hard to find, so I can't let go. Baby I'll be your one and only and you'll be mine...

We only got one life to live so let's ride it out together two hearts that beat as one ready and down for what ever. Don't be discouraged by my past cause we are not looking back. My main concern is you and I getting my life back on track...

Late nights we are sharing laughs while soaking in a bubble bath I wash your back and you wash mine. Later you're way deep in this ass, you watch me as I fall asleep kiss me good night on my cheek and thank GOD for delivering you a woman so sweet...

2/04   Anice Austin

Poetry in Motion

*I am a beautiful person both inside and out. I am truly **NOT** vain. I just appreciate what God has blessed me with. And you will too do the same. When I become your wifey. You'll make time for me; it's the little things that mean so much and this you soon shall see. A gentle kiss in the morning, the birthday card sent via express mail, the passionate love making that always drives you crazy, the footsie playing under the dinner table at one of the finest restaurants in town. The way I say... "I Love You" is what puts your heart at ease, the way I tease your body parts, and make you beg OH PLEASE!! You're willing to be my husband; I don't know what to say...the only thing I'm thinking of is when is the wedding day?! I want what you want and all of this is true everyone will be so happy on the day we say "I DO..." you opened up your heart to me and offered me a new life the way that folk should... but trust and believe on our honeymoon, you'll be screaming*

OH BABY YES THAT'S GOOD!!!

There is something about the letters to me that tell me you're sincere…you've shined a light on my darkest day, now my heart beats loud and clear. You've come into my life and my heart is overjoyed… I never again have to worry about that place that was hollow and void.

2/2004 Anice Austin

A Good Woman

*A good woman will captivate your mind,
and make your heart skip a beat.
A good woman knows the love she's aching to feel
for you is not quite complete.
A good woman has marveled at your letters
although short they are sweet...
A good woman wants love from you, she wants
everything, and she wants all you got. Nothing else
can compete.
To be totally honest with you, you've got this good
woman on the spot and that's real deep.
I'm telling you right now, I am a good woman,
ya heard!
Who'll stick by you 110% no matter what, good,
bad, indifferent, and never leave you hanging and
that's my word.
There is something about you, she has no doubt,
since she's such a good woman you,
She can't live without.
She cooks, cleans, keeps house
And tends to her man.
There's no way in the world he'd ever
have to use his hand.*

His woman's at home Life is just too sweet...
She massages her man from head to feet.
Being such a good woman I can't understand...
Why in the world she's been so long with out a man???

5/2004
By Anice Austin

Promise

My heart just aches everyday,

For the love that went away…

I've opened up my heart to you,

To place inside a love that's new…

You'll never understand in me,

The pain and anguish and misery …

You've promised to love me in future years,

You've promised to wipe away all my tears…

This love of ours will grow and grow,

You've promised a love like I'll never know…

You've promised me a carefree, joyous life

You've also promised I'd be your wife…

My heart is yours to keep, as long as

You can deal with me, a realness that's deep…

Anice `04

Things to think about

Think about the people you call your friends,
The people that claim they are there to the end.
Think about the worries you have in the day,
Think about the things you've been meaning to say.
Think about the loved ones, who have passed along the way,
Think about the ones that think they are here to stay.
Think about the pain that some may cause,
Think about the people that say you have flaws.
Think about the life you have set out to make,
Think about the children that DHS will try to take.
Think about the way you try to save what is yours,
Think about the hurt that seeps through your pores.
There are a lot of things to think about in this life,
Wondering all the while would you have made a good wife?
These are some of the things I think about,
It makes my head hurt so bad it makes me want to shout!!
Think about the things that make you "you".
Think about the things that make you blue.
GOD has blessed us with the process to think,
Use it don't abuse it; keep it safe so we don't lose it.

A. Austin   4/02/2008

A Black President

Here is something we never thought,
No more sneeking and fear of being caught...
Hurry, hurry don't be late, November fourth 2008.
This is the day that we won't forget
If my father were alive he'd be proud I just bet.
Martin Luther King and Rosa Park
Walked and marched for this day to come.
These are presents that are heven sent
Barack Obama first Black Predisent!
For the fact that the issues are crap,
We know he had nothing to do with that.
We will show them how it is done,
How to manage money and when the west was won.
This is a world of nothing but change
Enjoy the ride we have a chance to rearrange.
I loveAmerica because it took a vote
And in it's choice, Barack Obama was so remote.
God bless America you have done good
The next four years he will do the best as he should.

Anice Austin November 2008

If he were here

If he were here, things would be so different, in a way that is hard to say,

If he were here, I would need no help; in understanding he shared the wealth...

If he were here this would be the day, he'd celebrate the brand new way...

Obama for President, Phillies winning the Series,

If he were here, all of these things, yes he'd be pleased...

If he were here, we would have been at the game, life to me will not be the same...

Since I have not heard his name...

Rev. George Austin Sr. was a great man;

He helped me with things no one else could understand...

Thank you lord for the father that you gave me,

I know he's proud of the woman I came to be.

College at last, at the age of 42,

It doesn't matter, you have made it through.

Anice Austin Nov. 2008

This Book is dedicated to

My Mom for helping with all of my achievements. My little sister Dana and my Baby brother Dwight I love you "D"... 10/21/2007

www.ingramcontent.com/pod-product-compliance
Lightning Source LLC
Chambersburg PA
CBHW031218090426
42736CB00009B/976